1

Born in the Trap

By: The New Mizz Luvli Black

UF
Mizz Luv

Having a dream is normal. Fulfilling all of your dreams is not. Being able to fulfill your dreams is something that most don't get to feel. And if you're not careful, you can allow the wrong people in your life that will cost you it all. ---- The New Mizz Luvli Black

Chapter One

"Well... I guess congratulations are in order Amy," the nurse said staring at me with this weird ass smile on her face. "It looks like you're about seven weeks pregnant."

"I'm sorry say what?"

Did she really just say that shit? This was not what I was expecting her to say. Pregnant? With a baby? Damn. I didn't see that coming.

Here I was coming to the doctor's office thinking that I was just had a stomach bug or something, and, this woman is sitting here looking me in my face telling me I'm pregnant. God's gotta be playing a joke on me. Pregnant? My mama is about to have a cow and two chickens when she finds out. I can just imagine what she's gonna say. To keep it real, I think this is something she's been waiting on to happen anyway. She keep speaking it into existence.

"You only 19 years old." "You dumb as hell to be trying to have a baby this early." "You too stupid to be lying on your back fucking with these lil boys." "Who gone help you take care of the baby?" "How you gone raise it?" "How you gone feed it?"

She would be hitting me with every question she could think of whenever she thought I was up to something. She was always fussing at me about what I'm doing and who I'm with. I think if it was up to her, my ass would be in the house every day.

I'm 19! I want to live my life. But she treats me like I'm so damn fragile. She says I'm book smart but don't have the common sense that God gave a tumbleweed. But she's wrong. At least I think so. I know that I look a lot older than what I actually am. I look like I'm in my twenties. But I know how to take care of myself. And I carry myself well.

I'm tired of hearing about how I'm too naive and fast and all of that. She thinks everybody and they mama is trying to take advantage of me. But all of my friends are like me. I mean, at least I'm just now getting pregnant at 19 and not 15 years old like some of my friends. My homegirl Keisha had her first baby when she was 14, and she got two kids now by two different niggas and she's the same age as me.

Besides, it's not like I asked to look this way. I was just blessed. I couldn't help it I stood out. See I'm dark-skinned. Like darker than most of the girls that I know. They all got the pretty high yellow skin and all that, but I am literally chocolate. My boyfriend said I look like an Egyptian goddess and that real queens of Egypt aren't the high yellow girls that they show on TV or that we read about in our school books. Truthfully, I got teased more about my chocolate skin than anything. It wasn't until I hit high school that I realize that me being dark skinned and having the pretty eyes and everything was a good thing. I had a grown woman's ass and titties and a baby face.

I didn't really have a lot of friends growing up because I was developing so early and getting attention from these little dumb ass guys but once I became a woman? I started getting more attention. And not just from boys but girls too. The girls knew I could get a nigga quick. I knew some of them was just kicking it so they could get some of my leftovers but, I didn't really care like that. It wasn't like I wasn't getting attention from other niggas. If a boy like me, I would make him buy me lunch, and then he'd have to buy my friends lunch too. I used my looks to my advantage. That was the point of being cute in school. I didn't see how my friends were using me. I just thought that I was being a good friend. But the minute I got boo'd up, it stopped. I guess I was being taken advantage of. At least that's what my mama says.

Truth is, I'd much rather be taken advantage of than constantly hearing her tell me how stupid I am, and how I fall for anything and all that other crazy shit that she be talking about. I'm not like that. I'm not out there hoeing around with a bunch of different niggas. I lost my virginity when I was 16 years old to this boy Raekwon. We went to the same school and had a few classes together and he was fine as hell too. I already knew how he got down though. He had messed with a lot of my friends and every broad knew he was that nigga. I didn't care that he was a dog. I just wanted to lose my virginity so that I could see what it was like. To keep it real, I wasn't really impressed.

Now the nigga that I started fuckin' with after him? Mike? Yeah, he was on a whole other level. He loved eating pussy. He was the first one to eat my pussy. That shit was the bomb! But, he was slow as hell. Like he just seemed real stupid. That's what I get for fuckin' with these little young niggas though. I mean, I'm not saying that I was that much more mature, but compared to some of my homegirls out here partying all the time, and having babies by different niggas, I felt like I was doing a whole lot better.

It was just a shame that I couldn't get my own mama to see it. I'm 19 years old. If I was so immature and so naive, I wouldn't have made it this long without getting pregnant. I really didn't have much of a choice though. She went and dragged my ass to the free clinic and got me on the pill when I was 15. Once I started getting a figure, she told me that she didn't want me out there fuckin' and bringing babies home.

But, sometimes I forgot to take the pill. Clearly. But I didn't think I missed that many. Well, at least I'm working and taking care of myself. I give a cut of my check to my mama so that she can pay bills and, I'm doing a lot better than some of the girls that I grew up with. They all living in welfare housing, and collecting checks from the government. But not me.

Right after high school, I lucked up and got a job working at the hospital. One of the ladies that went to church with my mama works there, and she told me that she could get me a job. So, a week after graduation, I started working in medical administration and have been working there for the last seven months. I love it. I'm making my own money, and, I stay fly. I got all the latest shit, which I didn't have growing up, and I stay slaying on these hoes.

But grown or not, my ass was scared as hell to tell my mama that I was pregnant. Yea I'm grown and all and legally she can't do shit to me, but I already know that she gone put on a show. She gone cuss me out, then pray for my soul, then tell me how I am making a terrible mistake. But I'm keeping my baby. It's not just my baby. It's Terry's too.

Oh she gone have a field day with that shit. She can't stand Terry, and she make sure to let everybody and they mama know. It's not all Terry's fault though. He said it would probably happen. I just disregarded it cause we have been fucking around for so long and nothing happened. But then again, I was on birth control so.

Terry don't sound bad right? My family don't like the fact that I fuck with him, but, I love him. According to my mama, Terry is Satan's Spawn sent solely on this Earth to fuck up my life. But, real talk, Terry is my man. Me and him been together for a good minute. I know he'll be happy when I tell him that I'm pregnant. At least I'm pregnant by a nigga that's going to be able to take care of me.

He's the first guy that really makes me feel like I'm important and like I matter. He don't be coming down on me about dumb shit like who I'm hanging around. He's been my world for the last six months. I don't see why he couldn't be excited. My man Terry is a boss. I just hope that the boss will be happy with another baby.

****

Chapter Two

I remember when I met Terry. I was at work one day, and we were busy as hell. It was supposed to be this big hurricane that was hitting the city so, people were calling out left and right. My ass was about to go home, but then they started offering double overtime so I figured what the hell?

I don't even think I was on the clock but an hour yet when he came in. He was with this pregnant girl, who I later found out was his baby mama. I didn't even think he paid me any attention until my shift was almost over and he came out in the lobby to use his phone. His loud ass was talking right in front of my desk and it was irritating me cause I couldn't hear.

"Excuse me sir," I said. "Do you mind stepping away from the desk to talk on the phone?"

He kept talking like he didn't hear me say anything to him.

"Sir," I warned again after a few more seconds. "You're talking kind of loud, so if you don't mind just stepping over there."

He turned around like he was about to pop off, but then broke out smiling.

"Aye my nigga let me hit you right back," he said to whoever was on the phone. "How you doing sweetheart?"

"I'm fine." I answered politely. I was not trying to lose my job over a random nigga.

"Yes you are," he smiled. "So what's your name?"

I know this nigga was not sitting here trying to holla at me and he came in there with his baby mama! I just glanced down at my name tag and gave him a look like "nigga please."

"So you got a man?" He asked.

"And that's your business why?" I said.

"Anything I want I make my business," he told me.

I had to give it to him, he was slick with it.

Terry stood a good six-foot-three, fine as hell, with this caramel complected skin. He wasn't a pretty boy or anything like that because his whole persona read "thug". You could tell that by looking at him. He was iced out and all of that. But, I was still cautious.

"So how's your girlfriend doing?" I asked.

"That ain't my girl," he told me without batting an eye. "That's my baby mama. But that's a cute way of asking me if you can be my girl."

He had this smile on his face that was so sneaky.

"It's not my business." I recovered quickly. "I don't know you."

"But you can know me," he said stepping towards me. "My name is Terry."

"Amy." I introduced myself.

"So Ms. Amy, why don't you let me get your number?"

I don't know why, but I felt myself blushing.

"Nah I think I'm cool." I shrugged him off. "Besides, your baby mama is in there giving birth and you out here trying to holler at another girl."

"Okay she my baby mama so what?" He said. "I got three other baby mamas but they ain't trippin'."

"What?" I asked.

"Yeah. I got three kids. And I take care of every last one of them," he said. "I ain't had no issues with no females yet."

Four kids by four different broads? What the fuck!

"So they just having your babies like that?" I pressed.

"Nah," he said. "It ain't nothing like that. But what's good you gone give me your number or not? Cause I do got to get back in there though."

I shook my head.

"I'm too young to be dealing with baby mama drama." I told him.

"How old are you?"

"I just turned 19." I told him proudly. "Damn you damn sure don't look it."

He was sizing me up and down. Even in scrubs, I was still thick as hell and nothing could have that ass. He could tell that he had me.

He reached over and grabbed the pen out of my cup holder and scribbled his number down on a piece of paper.

"Call me tomorrow. I'm gone take you to lunch."

He put the pen down on top of paper and walked off without another word and I was left standing there drooling. I didn't even realize that people were watching until my boss came over and poked me in the side.

"Girl don't you mess with that boy," she warned. "He's too much for you."

She was right, but I was already curious.

I called him the next day and I really didn't expect him to answer considering he just had a baby, but, we ended up talking on the phone, and he came and took me out to lunch just like he said he would. After that, we started kicking it heavy. I found out he was 40 years old, had four kids by four different women, but I didn't care about any of that. He treated me like I was the only woman in the world. And he spoiled me rotten.

He asked me about my dreams, and he helped me make them come true. I had a hair salon I was running within 2 months of us being together. Of course, he was using the shop to clean his money through, but he put it in my name so that way if something happened I wouldn't get in trouble. I was 19 with a bank account that had more figures than Jennifer Hudson on American Idol. Terry wanted me to quit working, but, I still wanted to be able to have my own money.

I left work nervous. Today was just so throwed. I was not planning on coming to work, passing out and finding out that I was pregnant. But, I definitely couldn't wait to tell Terry. I drove home and texted him to let him know to meet me at my house. Oh yeah did I mention that my man bought me a house? Yea. How many 19 year olds do you know that got a damn house in they name? But I had bigger fish to fry.

By the time I got to the house, my stomach was in knots. Terry already had four kids, so I didn't know how he was going to react. But, I know I didn't make the baby by myself. When he got there, I tried to be cute about it and let him guess but, I just flat out told him after so long and he was cool with it. He didn't really have much of a reaction. He just told me that once I had the baby that I would need to quit working. So, I was good.

I fucked up and told my momma that I was pregnant, and she changed her number. But, it was fine. I wasn't going to sweat it. I kept grinding. I worked every day of my pregnancy up until the day that I had our son. I was good because I had everything that I wanted and needed. I had a house, I was making money out the shop in about to open up a clothing store, I had a nigga that was respected in the streets plus loves the hell out of me and I had Jr.

Life was sweet. The only issue that I had was the baby mama drama, and Terry kept that shit out of our situation because he didn't want me stressing while I was pregnant. He meant what he said about none of his baby mamas giving him problems. If they did, I didn't know about it. But that shit didn't last long.

You know how they say that everything that that glitters ain't gold? Believe it. Cause all along I thought I had 24 Karat when really it was just Fool's Gold.

****

Chapter Three

"I'm sorry what did you just say?"

I heard the words come out of his mouth, but I just couldn't process it.

"You heard what I said," he replied dryly. "Don't start this dramatic bullshit."

"What the hell you mean don't start no bullshit?" I shrieked. "You just told me you got another bitch pregnant. Some other hoe is about to have your baby!"

I was so mad that the tears were just streaming down my face. I was used to females being in my man's face because he was one of the most paid drug dealers in Florida and chicks was always in his face but this? This was too much.

"What you want me to say huh?" he asked. "Amy you know how it is when I'm out here in these streets. You know how these hoes can be."

"Obviously I don't know Terry." I told him.

This nigga was acting like he just told me that he was going out of town or some shit. He was having a baby by another woman. I had just given birth less than a week ago to our son and walking around here thinking that we going to get married and all this, on some white folks "ride off into the sunset" type shit, and he drops this bomb on me.

"What's her name?" I asked.

"You don't know her," he said walking past me and heading into the kitchen.

I followed right behind his ass.

"You don't know who I know." I snapped. "Now what's her name?"

He gave me an annoyed look as he went through the refrigerator for a soda.

"Deborah."

"So how long you been fucking her?" I pried.

"Why we still talking about this shit?" he sighed.

"Because you just came up in here a WEEK after your son was born and tell me that you have ANOTHER baby on the way!" I screamed. "That's why we still talking about this shit. Nigga my muthafuckin pussy ain't even heal yet and you already on to the next bitch! And if she pregnant, that means you was fucking with her before I had Junior. So… you been playing me?"

"You need to lower your voice before you wake him up," he warned.

"Nigga fuck you! I'm the one up with him all night anyway." I reminded him. "You need to tell her to get rid of it."

"Don't fuckin try that shit with me," he snapped. "You know how

16

it is. You know I don't believe in that abortion shit. Now she having my baby so it is what it is."

He looked at me like he wanted to choke my ass out for even suggesting such a thing.

I felt like Terry had just punched me in my damn stomach or something. Especially the way he was acting like what he just revealed to me was nothing. I mean he was right. He was out in the streets a lot and hoes did want him but, I didn't think that he would actually be out there fucking around with everybody either. How could he say that he loved me when he was out here making babies with other bitches.

"So you sure this baby is yours?" I asked him after several minutes of silence.

I was really trying to hold it together but the shit was hard.

He gave me this look like I asked him if he had a third arm or something.

"I mean what Terry?" I stressed. "You talking bout how it is out here in the streets. Apparently, every bitch out here tryna get at you. But you out here fucking these hoes obviously without a condom and shit, not giving a fuck about the fact that I just gave birth to your son!"

I was pissed off. I couldn't believe how he was making me look and I was just going the hell off.

"So if it's really like that out there in the streets, how you know this hoe ain't tryna trap you with somebody else's baby?" I pushed.

"Cause she not," he answered bluntly. "Trust me."

"Trust you?" I laughed. "How the hell can I trust you. You just told me that you got another bitch pregnant Terry. Hello? How the hell am I supposed to trust you?"

Clearly his ass wasn't realizing what the hell he was saying. Or he just didn't care. Either way, it was pissing me off because he was being so cocky about the shit.

It was in that moment that I thought about my mother's warning. I could just hear her saying how naïve and stupid I was for believing that this nigga wanted to be with me on some serious shit like that.

I played myself. I should have known that his ass wasn't going to be able to just be with one girl. But I couldn't leave to go back to my mother. I couldn't go home with a baby and tell her that she was right. I would have much rather put up with him then deal with that. If I loved him and didn't trip, he would see that I was loyal to him and he would be loyal to me.

So I stayed.

Of course, Terry tried to apologize with gifts, and I took them. Believe it or not, I actually met this Deborah chic and made it clear that the only reason I wasn't dragging her ass is cause she was pregnant with Terry's baby. She surprised me though cause she didn't really fuck with Terry like that and had just fucked up her birth control and got pregnant. She wasn't trying to get at him and only talked to him when it came to their baby so, she was cool with me.

She gave birth to a little girl six months later and I felt some type of way but, I made it work. Terry promised me that he was done fucking around and that I was all that mattered to him, and I made sure of it; well, the best I could.

Deborah was cool. I mean shit, I couldn't fault her for some shit that he did. It was his fault for not telling her that he had a girl. She was pretty much the only thing that I had to a friend. I even gave her a job at the salon.

"Girl, you lucky you got Terry doing all of this for you," she would say.

Yeah Terry bought me the salon and everything, but I worked hard to keep everything running. I missed being at work. I was at home all the time with Junior, and Terry was still out hustling. It was lonely, and my mind always got the better of me. I was always wondering what Terry was doing and who he was doing it with.

I didn't have to wonder for too long because as much as I believed that he had only cheated once and really meant that he wasn't going to fuck around on me again, once again, he showed me who he really was. He had fucked three other bitches after Deborah. Every time I found out about a new chick, I would find myself confronting her ready to fuck her up, and all Terry would do is apologize and buy me some shit to try to shut me up. After a while though, he stopped doing that. He just stopped caring. It was becoming almost routine for me to find out that he was fucking with some girl.

I don't know what it was but one day I just snapped. One night he came home smelling like straight up Bath & Body Works spray. Enough was enough.

He walked his happy ass right past me and the baby and I just lost it.

"So you just going to walk your black ass in the house and not even speak to me or your son?" I snapped.

He turned and looked at me and sighed.

"Yo, who the fuck you think you're talking to?" He asked.

"I'm talking to you!" I yelled. "Or did you think you were talking to one of your other bitches?"

"Here we go again with this bullshit," he said. "Why the fuck you questioning me and shit? Damn Amy, you ain't my wife, and you ain't my fuckin mama."

"So cause I'm not your wife, I can't ask where the fuck you been?" I replied. "So you can just disrespect me?"

"Disrespect?" he laughed. "Yo, you taken care of, you got shit that other bitches don't have, and you good. So what the fuck you got to complain for?"

"Are you serious right now Terry?" I asked. "What you mean why am I complaining? You out here cheating on me. You KEEP saying you sorry but you KEEP doing it!"

I was breaking down. I don't even think I understood what I was saying I was crying so hard.

"Everything that my mama said about you was true!" I sniffed. "You played me. You did!"

He just looked at me and took a sip of his beer leaning against the counter looking at me like I was speaking a foreign language.

"What I did was changed your life," he spoke. "Look around you Amy. Look at everything you got. Shit, you ain't even 30 yet and got a fucking house, cars, money, businesses and shit. All thanks to me."

He started pacing back and forth and I listened trying to figure out where the hell he was going with this.

"I mean damn! You so worried about the next bitch that you can't even focus on the shit that you got right in front of you," he raged. "Do you see any of them other hoes up in here living like this? No. A nigga out here handling business. Yea I fucked up. I fucked around when I probably shouldn't have. But shit, sometimes a nigga get fucked up and do some stupid shit. But I come home to you!"

Ain't this some shit?

"So what? I'm supposed to be grateful and ignore the fact that my man just goes out here and fucks whoever he wants because he got me all of this shit and comes home to me?" I questioned. "I don't give a fuck about you buying me a house or these businesses or cars and shit. I mean damn, you treat me like I'm one of these groupies or something instead of your girl." I added. "But no, because it's Terry, the nigga that know how to hustle and get money, I'm supposed to just accept everything else that you do. I can't do that no more."

I wanted to hit him in the head with the fucking bottle that he was holding he was pissing me off so bad. It was my turn to pace the floor.

"Every time I turn around, it's a different broad in my face telling me how she done fucked my man. That's humiliating as fuck and I'm your woman!"

I didn't know what else to say to him to get him to understand. It was like talking to a brick wall.

"Look man, I ain't got time for all this drama," he sighed.

He threw the bottle away and walked right past me. He had made it clear. I meant nothing to him. All I was to him was just another baby mama.

The next day, he got up and left to hit the streets as usual, and I packed everything that I had, I got my son, and I got the hell out of there. I left his ass a nice little letter letting him know that everything that he got me he could have. Since it seemed like all he cared about was what he did for me instead of how he hurt me, he can keep all that shit.

I know mama thought I was naïve and dumb but, I had some sense about me. I had saved up money and had a little "rainy day" fund from the several transactions from the bank.

Even though the businesses were in my name, he controlled a lot of the money as far as the accounts. I had opened up a separate account he knew nothing about and had continuous deposits going in, especially after I found out about Deborah.

When I left, of course he threatened to stop funding everything. It was fine by me because I could handle it on my own even though he wanted me to fail. I kept one of the cars though because let's keep it real, I did have his son and I wasn't going to walk away with anything empty-handed.

I got a nice house to rent, and was officially done with him. We still talked because we had Junior, and at the end of the day I wasn't going to keep his son from him, but, as far as he and I was concerned, it was over.

Of course, he was constantly reminding me that I wasn't going to be able to make it without him, but I did. I got my old job back working at the hospital, and I was doing okay.

My luck got even better when I met Kenneth. Kenneth and I hooked up briefly, but we realized we were better off as friends. But, thanks to Kenneth, I had a little side business going on besides working at the hospital. See Kenneth was from New York and had the biggest hook up when it came to the shoes and clothes. So, he and I became business partners of sorts.

I would buy the shoes from him at a cheap price and turn around and sell them at almost three times the amount that I bought them for. I was that bitch! Medical assistant by day and hustler by night. I hustled everything out of the trunk of my car. I didn't need Terry no matter what he said!

****

Chapter Four

After Terry and I broke up, I spent damn near a year on the dating scene meeting men. It was just too much. Every guy that I met was just like him or trying to be like him. They were all about themselves, or, they just wanted me to fuck them and stroke their egos.

I wasn't at that point in my life anymore. I couldn't understand why it was so hard to meet a man that was on the same level that I was. Every guy that I met, within a couple of days, they would come at me with some bullshit, and rather than waste my time, I just dismissed them and went right back to being single. I know I was going to have to kiss a few frogs to get my prince but damn!

I remember I met Paul. Paul was a wannabe pimp. He was way too much like Terry, to the point where he felt like he could try to tell me what to do. He didn't last long at all.

Then there was Justin. Justin was cool, but he was really young and spent a lot of his time playing video games or eating fucking cereal. It was like dating a frat boy or some shit.

And then there was Elijah. I don't know what the hell I was thinking about with him. He was too much of a pretty boy. He spent more time in the damn mirror than I did.

Ladies fair warning. Anytime you meet a nigga that's fucking gorgeous as hell with the silky hair and all that, just know that he's more of a pretty boy and is more concerned about his looks then you are about yours.

I was about to give up on the dating scene when I met Thomas. He made me have hope; well, for a while.

I had been working back at the hospital for almost a year, and things were going good. Terry was still around for Junior as far as making sure that his child support was paid. We had minimal conversation with each other because Terry was still being Terry, meaning he was being an asshole. But aside from that, that first year was hell.

I remember when I met him. I wasn't into my job anymore, and I decided one day that I would just quit. I was bored, and I just felt like I didn't want to be there.

"Girl what's wrong with you?" My coworker Angel asked.

"I'm just tired of being here." I confessed. "Like when I first started working here, I was so excited. I loved this job. But now, I swear to God I can't stand coming in here sometimes."

"Well damn," she smirked. "Nice to know how you really feel."

I rolled my eyes and sucked my teeth at her.

"Girl hush." I said. "You know it ain't you or nothing. It's just... I don't know. I thought that I would be much further in my life right now. Honestly, I'm making more money hustling shoes than I am working in here."

"Okay so why don't you just do that full-time?" She asked.

"That's a good point." I admitted.

Thinking about it, it made sense. I was doing a lot of business with my shoes and everything. The thing about it was, I just didn't want to be in Florida anymore.

"I think I wanna move." I told her.

"Where?" She asked.

"I think I'm going to move to Georgia." I answered. "That's the spot where it seems like everything is happening. I got some friends up there anyway. They went for school and everyone has been telling me how nice it is when I talk to them."

"Girl you know your baby daddy gone have a fit when he find out you tryna move," she said.

I forgot how much everybody else seemed to respect that nigga but me.

"Girl, I don't give a fuck what he gotta say." I huffed. "I'm doing this for me and for mine. He'll still be able to see Junior and everything. I'm not keeping him from him. But, I gotta move if I wanna do this big."

"I guess," she said. "But you know we gonna miss you here!"

She started hugging on me and I giggled.

"I know." I smiled. "I'ma miss your crazy self too."

That was the moment that changed everything for me.

I went to my boss and I gave her my two-week notice and as soon as I could, I was out. I packed everything up, and I told Terry that I was moving me and Junior to Georgia.

He tried to make it seem like I was taking his son from him, but on the real, it wasn't like he spent time with him anyway.

"My nigga you can write a check and mail it anywhere." I told him when he tried to jump down my throat.

26

"Oh you think you funny now?" He snapped. "So you just gone take my son and leave thinking that the shit is cool?"

"Okay Terry, when was the last time you actually spent time with your child?" I asked. "Seriously. When was it huh? He's damn near three years old, and you seen him what? Maybe five or six times? A check is only going to do but so much. I can give him that anywhere."

I don't know why this nigga thought I still had to answer to him.

"Yeah whatever," he growled dropping it.

I swear I regret the day that I ever met this nigga; much less had a baby with his ass. But, all of that was about to be a distant memory.

I moved to Georgia, I found me a nice house, and after about a month of looking for the perfect space, I opened up a nice little shoe store.

Lets not forget about Thomas. I met him in Florida but he lived in Georgia. And no, I didn't move for him. He was an accountant that was helping me with the financing for the store and everything. He was gorgeous. I was a little leery at first because of the track record that my ass seemed to have meeting men, but, he was really sweet. He came off shy almost. Plus I knew he had a good job because hell in a sense he was working for me.

He did everything that a man should do when they first meet a woman. He wined me, and he dined me. After a while, when I saw that he was a good guy, I introduced him to Junior and he liked him. Everything was perfect with us. That's where things went wrong. I got too comfortable.

We'd been dating for about six months and everything was going really good. One random August afternoon turned me bitter. He had spent the night at the house and was heading to the office and I was heading to the store to go do some paperwork and whatnot.

I still remember seeing the young chick walk through the door. She couldn't have been more than maybe 21. She came in rocking some college gear from Spelman. I really didn't pay her any attention at first because a lot of young girls came into my store to buy shoes. The store wasn't far from one of the bigger colleges and I made a lot of my money off of them.

Erica, one of the newer employees that I hired greeted her and was helping her out. She had several pair that she was trying on and I was kind of keeping an eye to make sure that she wasn't just wasting time. It wasn't until I was hanging around the cash register that I even noticed it. The girl had about six pair of shoes that she was buying.

She had put her phone down to pay for them, when I saw her screensaver. I was so confused because I could swear it was Thomas on it. At first, I thought I was tripping, but the more I looked, the more I knew that it was him.

I didn't even know what to say. The breath had been snatched from my body. I tried to play it cool, because I didn't want her to think I was just staring at her like some crazy woman.

"I like your phone." I complimented.

"Thank you," she replied as she waited for Erica to finish bringing her up. "This is like the third one that I had to get because I keep cracking my screen."

"Girl you better get a phone case for that thing," Erica chimed in.

"I am. My boyfriend told me the same thing. He said he's not buying me no more phones."

"I know that's right." Erica laughed.

"Damn girl your daddy is cute." I chimed in going back to the picture.

I was praying that it was her daddy and that this nigga hadn't gone and fucked some Disney Princess. I needed it to be the case.

"Girl that ain't my daddy," she laughed. "More like my sugar daddy."

My heart had sunk to my stomach at this point. I couldn't stand bitches like her.

"Damn girl!" Erica grinned.

"Yeah that's my boyfriend Thomas," the little bitch bragged.

"How you pull that?"

Erica was getting on my nerves with her nosey ass. See this is why I was glad that I left my personal life separate from my employees. Good thing is they didn't know a damn thing about me other than I was the bitch to sign their paychecks.

"Well he's definitely cute." I told her dryly.

I wanted to knock her little young ass on the floor but, I had to maintain composure.

"Yeah. My mama was right."

I frowned at her not sure what the hell she meant.

"She told me that there are five types of men that you need in your life," she started to explain.

Oh I had to hear this shit.

"You need the Mandingo. That's the one that's fuckin you good. You got to have a main man. That's the little boyfriend that you take out and about," she continued. "Then you gotta have a gay boy, you tell all your secrets to him. You got the sugar daddy to give you the money that you need, and then you got the ugly one to watch your kids."

She and Erica were both laughing like the shit was hella funny. Thomas was messing around with a chick like this? I was done. Hearing that just turned my stomach. I can't believe I wasted all of this time with him.

After she and Erica giggled with each other, she left and I reprimanded Erica's ass for being to personal with the customers. It took everything in me not to break down in tears, especially after listening to Erica's ass complimenting her and talking about how she needed to get on her level.

This is the kind of shit that I had to compete with? The fact that I even had to feel like I had to compete with another bitch like I wasn't enough for him.

It wasn't even that I was upset about this stupid broad fucking him because at the end of the day, it was about what he did. I just couldn't understand why I kept meeting the wrong type of dudes. What was I putting out there? What was I not seeing? This is the second time that I was into somebody and they cheated on me. What is so wrong with me?

Maybe it's just not meant for me to be with anybody. That shit is only for TV and romance books. Cause every nigga is going to stick his dick in something else if he gets opportunity. And clearly, Thomas was no different. Well fuck it and fuck him.

Chapter Five

Ladies if you pay attention to nothing else, pay attention to me on this.

A man, is just out for himself. Ain't one man walking on this Earth that's going to really be about you before himself.

After that bullshit that I went through with Thomas, I became withdrawn. I didn't want to be involved with or fuck with anybody. All I was about was my money and my son. I had vested years into my baby daddy with his trifling ass, only to turn around and do the shit again with a nigga that I actually thought I may potentially have something with.

But you know the funniest shit? I never even told him that I was done with him. I never even confronted him about the little young ass girl that was all up in my shit. He called me later that day, and I just told him I couldn't be with him anymore. I didn't wait for a response. I just told him it was over and hung up the phone.

Of course, he was blowing up my phone and trying to pop up at the store and shit, but, one thing about me, when I'm done, I'm done. I had to train myself to be that way after my drama with Terry's ass.

I wasn't about to be in a relationship with him only for him to turn around and do the same shit that Terry's ass did. So ladies, you better take heed to that warning of "once a cheater always a cheater." No matter how much they may say that they not going to do it again, or how they not that type of nigga, don't believe that bullshit! Because that's exactly what the fuck it is; bullshit.

Or maybe it's just me. I don't know. But, I know after that mess, being single was the life I wanted. I didn't want to be bothered with anybody. It was just too complicated. I had male friends don't get me wrong. You know a girl has to get her little itch scratched every now and then. That's how me and Demetrius got involved.

He and I had been cool when we were both in school in Florida. He never really paid me attention like that because he always had a damn flock of groupies around him. I wasn't anywhere near his level. He tried to holla but, I knew he had messed with some of my friends and I was scared they would hate me and I wouldn't have any friends so, it never happened.

I knew he had come to Georgia for school a while back but, never knew that he stayed. Demetrius was going to be big. He played ball, and was fine as hell, but of course back in the day I was too caught up on Terry's ass to even really look at him like that.

It wasn't until I ran into him at a McDonald's that I realized how damn fine he really was. I laughed because he was spitting game not even realizing he knew me. I had walked into the McDonald's because I had to pee really bad and the line was extremely long in the Drive-Thru.

I was running so hard I almost knocked him over.

"Watch where the hell you going!" He snapped.

"My bad." I apologized in passing.

I still wasn't really noticing anything because like I said, I had to pee. When I finished and came back out, he was standing in line and I apologized to him again.

"You straight," he said as he started looking me up and down and licking his lips.

I guess it was me looking at him crazy that made him a little nervous.

"What's good?" He asked.

"I don't know I feel like I've seen you somewhere before." I said.

"Nah baby girl. Trust me I'd remember seeing that gorgeous face of yours."

I rolled my eyes. This nigga was so corny.

"What's your name?" He asked.

"Amy." I answered.

I was regretting speaking to him at this moment. I started looking at the menu like I didn't plan on getting a damn Happy meal for my son.

"Well I'm Demetrius."

My eyes got big as hell.

"Now I know why you look familiar." I smirked. "Did you used to go to Dorsey High School?"

He took a couple of steps back and looked me up and down again.

"Damn!" He smiled. "Amy? Is it really you?"

"Yes." I laughed.

"Yo you look good!" he complimented. "Yeah I remember that Chris told me you was going to be moving out here when I talked to him a while back."

"Yeah good old Chris." I murmured.

Chris was another friend that went to school with us and lived in Georgia. He and I talked all the time. It's no wonder that Demetrius name hadn't come up before.

"Yeah I moved here a little bit ago. Me and my son." I told him.

"Oh word? I ain't know you had a kid."

"Yeah." I smiled. "That's my little man."

"That's wassup," he grinned.

He was looking at me like I was on the damn menu. I ain't gone lie though. He was looking real tasty. My hormones was jumping.

"We'll look I ain't gone hold you up or nothing. Why don't you give me your number and I'll hit you up and we can link up?" he suggested.

"Okay." I agreed and gave him my number.

I didn't really think much into it because Demetrius was the homie. I knew him from back in the day, and my mindset wasn't on hooking up. When he called me to get up, I figured we would be getting up to hang out and catch up, which I really had fun doing but, I never really knew that he had ulterior motives. I guess I just didn't pay attention to the warning signs.

After a couple of weeks of us texting and hanging out and stuff, he was finding his way to my house more than I wanted to see him, and each time would be later in the evening. I didn't have a problem with it or anything, but, it was like he was trying to wife me. I made it clear from jump that I wasn't trying to be with anybody, because I wasn't trying to put myself out there again to get hurt. Plus, it wasn't a good luck to keep bringing niggas around Junior. He didn't need that.

He said that he understood so, it was easy to just hang out with him and kick it, reminiscing about the old days. It was something about him. He was different. He gave me so much attention, and I needed that. I needed a man to make me feel special. But I just didn't want to rush anything.

Well you know what happened next right? I started fucking him. And baby! When I tell you Demetrius' stroke game is something vicious!

The first time that we had sex, I promise you that nigga ate my pussy so good that every piece of my heart and soul was taken with the drops of juice that he sucked from my body. I felt like at one point my soul was floating around the room looking down at me clapping with excitement.

It happened so damn fast I still don't know how we took it that far.

One night, he had come over to hang out after one of his photo shoots. We were watching Jungle Fever one minute, and it was the scene where Wesley Snipes had old girl bent over the desk fucking the hell out of her. The next thing I know, he's sucking and biting on my neck and that shit felt hella good! My pussy was screaming!

I was in that bitch moaning and trying to stay quiet so I didn't wake Junior, but, his body pressed against mine felt so good.

"I've been wanting to taste you so bad," he whispered as he licked on my neck. "Sitting over here looking all fine and shit."

All I could do was nod my head.

He stood me up and stripped me down out of my clothes and started kissing me all over. My body was on fire! I whimpered, and I could see him grinning with pleasure. He knew he had my ass.

"Oh shit!" I moaned.

The further that he spread my legs, the more that my pussy opened up, and he devoured me like I had been starving him.

I felt like I had met my match with Demetrius. The dick was indescribable. I think I must have cum at least five or six times from him eating my pussy before we actually started fucking. When he slid that dick inside of me, she responded like the Venus flytrap. Them lips latched onto him and my walls started contracting and convulsing. This nigga was fucking me like he had some shit to prove.

I finally remembered how to speak and cried out.

"Please Demetrius!"

This nigga laughed at me.

"Please what?" he taunted. "Please go deeper? Huh?"

He dug deeper in me and I hissed.

"Please what?" he kept on. "Please go faster?"

He started thrusting in and out of me and the back of my couch was hitting the wall.

"Please what?" he repeated now biting at my nipples and looking me in the eyes. "What you want me to do? I thought I was pleasing you?"

I couldn't say shit. All that could escape from my mouth were the sounds of me cummin.

I don't know if he was on that Henny dick or what, but his ass didn't cum for damn near an hour.

"You know you aren't fucking normal!" I heaved as he fucked the dog shit out of me.

Oh a bitch was gone! Why I never fucked with Demetrius before I don't know. But I had that good shit with him.

I mean Demetrius had me fucked up, down, left, right, and all around like a fucking compass. And that itself is a gang of trouble. Because the niggas that know that they got good dick, are the main ones you got to watch out for. They know how to use that shit to get what they want, and the way that Demetrius was slinging it, he was planning on getting it all.

****

Chapter Six

Demetrius was giving it to me on a regular but as good as it was, it was things that I was starting to notice.

I've never met a man that was wanting to be with somebody so bad. No matter how much I told him I wasn't ready for a relationship, he would always have something to try to convince me otherwise; usually his dick.

"Baby you just ain't met the right nigga yet," he would say while he was inside me.

Or he would tell me that he didn't like us just fucking around and giving his pussy away knowing that would turn me on. Why? Because usually he was digging me out when he would say that. But I wasn't going to fold. I was too guarded.

He came over one night to hang out and we ended up having one of our many all-out fuck sessions that left both of us happy and hungry.

"Damn." I said rolling over and curling up to get some sleep.

"So when we gone go ahead and make this official?" he asked. "I can't keep giving you the grade A dick and shit all raw."

He was really starting to get on my nerves with the shit. Didn't nobody tell his ass to stop wearing condoms. I was on birth control cause I wasn't going to be having nobody's baby no time soon. This shit was starting to get old.

"Demetrius we done been over this shit before." I sighed. "I told you I'm not tryna be in no relationship with nobody like that right now so why you keep asking?"

I was trying not to sound so agitated but, it was getting redundant and I was getting tired of it.

I guess it didn't work cause he started acting like he was all mad and everything.

"Man that shit don't make no sense," he huffed. "Shit a nigga over here every day and shit and we doing every damn thing mufuckas do in a relationship. So what? You just tryna have a relationship without the title?"

"I didn't say that." I said.

At this point I had turned to face him because I was about to put his ass out.

"Look D, I told you between my son, and work, and opening up this second store, my time for a relationship is limited." I reminded him. "Hell you see the only real time I can do anything is late. And I ain't tryna have no relationship like that. It's not fair to either one of us. Plus, honestly, I just don't wanna get too involved and get played."

I had a right to feel that after everything that I had been through.

"I just want to just take time to be single, and focus on the store and make sure I set a good example for Junior." I explained. "I hope you understand that."

"Yea," he answered with an attitude rolling his eyes.

I wasn't trying to hurt him but this is exactly why I didn't want to be with nobody. All this damn arguing and stuff. He sitting in here with an attitude and all I wanted to do was sleep.

"I'm not saying that I'm never gonna want to be in a relationship with you. Just not right now."

He just sat looking like he wasn't giving a fuck as to what I was saying.

"Maybe we should cool out for a little bit." I told him.

He looked at me for a few seconds and got up and started to get dressed.

This shit was too much. Why was this shit so damn complicated? My ass needed to go to a convent or something.

I'm tired of niggas making me feel guilty like I did something wrong.

"D, you don't have to go right now." I said trying to smooth things over. "I'm not saying just get up and walk out in this instant."

"I might as well," he finally spoke. "On some real shit Amy, you on that bullshit. You know how many broads would be tripping over themselves to be with me and you over here acting like you doing me a favor."

Oh my god are you serious right now?

"You making way too much out of this." I stressed. "All I'm saying is I'm not trying to be tied down to nobody right now because I got a lot going on. I done had nigga hurt me, cheat on me, use me and I'm just not trying to do that again."

"So I'm just supposed to deal with the shit that another nigga did," he spat.

"You don't have to do anything." I snapped. "But you acting like you God Almighty talking bout how I should be lucky that you want to be with me ain't helping either. That's some shit my ex has said."

He was only making it worse for himself. If he was going to come at me with some bullshit then I was going to give it right back to him.

"You wanna sit here and act like I'm just supposed to be thankful that you chose me or something."

"C'mon man I ain't mean it like that," he said. "I'm just saying Amy, you different than the other chicks I been with. You special. You the type of chick that a nigga wanna bring home to his mama.

You carry yourself a different way than most of these broads out here. You been through some shit like you keep harping on and shit yea but, you got your own. A real nigga like me would support you and be there for you baby. You deserve that."

My heart softened a little bit when he said that. No man had ever really told me anything like that before. The closest thing I got to flattery was with Terry and we see how that shit turned out.

Maybe it wouldn't be so bad to give him a chance. He walked over towards me and grabbed my hand in his.

"Just give me the chance to show you that every nigga ain't out here tryna do you wrong baby," he whispered. "Let me be the first man that makes you feel like you're worth everything that you are."

Hearing that, how could I not want to be with him?

We spent the rest of the night making love and the shit was amazing as always.

Silly of me. I should have listened to my gut. Because I was so wrapped up in the things that he was saying, I just ignored all of the signs that were right there in front of my ass the whole time. What possible reason could this man have to want to be up under me so much?

The next morning, he left to go handle some business, and I got onto my computer to respond to some emails and do some research on this store that I was opening up in Decatur. I don't know what it was, but, something was just nagging at me. As much as I tried to ignore it, I couldn't anymore.

No more than maybe ten minutes after I started responding to emails and everything, that nagging voice won and I said fuck it. I typed in Demetrius' name into Google and so much shit came up that I had to filter to make sure that I was not pulling up more than one person. This man was basically a fucking Gigolo!

Not only was his name coming up under lawsuits from other women that claimed that he ripped them off, but, his so-called modeling career had failed, and businesses that he bragged on were nonexistent.

I couldn't help but to sit back in shock. I was with a total pathological liar! I felt like the dumbest woman on the planet. Here I was thinking that he really wanted to be with me, when it was my motherfucking money that he was after. That had to be the only reason that he was fucking with me.

I looked at all this shit about lawsuits from women, plus child support that he's paying. Everything started to make sense. All of those times that he would come over, and he would wait until damn near two or three in the morning before he would decide to go home knowing that I would tell him to just stay over.

Here I am telling him to stay at the house cause I didn't want him driving that late being tired, and this nigga just didn't have nowhere to go. He's staying up under me all the damn time because I'm the one taking care of his ass.

I was sitting there thinking about it and this nigga got right under me and played my ass like lotto. I'm giving him money, buying him clothes; hell, he was right! We did have a relationship without the title.

I'm so busy telling him that I don't want to be with him, that I didn't even realize I'm already supporting this nigga. The shit was beyond crazy.

"I can't believe this shit." I said to myself. "I'm really convinced that I just got a dark cloud hanging over me or something. Like God you must really be having some fun right now because I swear everytime I try to stay away from the same type of dude, here he come in a different wrapper!"

I started logging on and checking my accounts and everything just hoping that he hadn't completely wiped me out. From what I read online, he had done it to quite a few females before me.

I could see that there were certain things that he must have bought because I would never spend $1,000 at a damn Foot Locker or $1,500 at Gucci. It was Demetrius.

Here he was bragging about how good he looked and getting these jobs, and it was because I was the one footing the bill. I felt like a fool. But, one thing was for damn sure, I had definitely learned how to handle my shit by now.

"I got something for your ass." I said to myself.

I spent the rest of the day canceling credit cards, and reported every card that I had stolen. He had been enjoying himself on my hard-earned money but that shit stopped right then. I was going to make sure that Demetrius ass wasn't taking advantage of me anymore.

Not even an hour later, I got a phone call from the Dekalb County jail.

"Hello?" I answered.

"Aye I need you to come bail me out of jail," he rushed.

"Why are you in jail?"

"Man I tried to use your credit card you let me hold a while back to get gas and the fucking card was declined. So I went into the damn store and they talking about it was reported stolen or some shit and they think I stole it," he explained.

"Oh yeah I know." I said slowly.

"What?" He asked.

"I said I know." I repeated. "I reported my card stolen."

"What the fuck Amy? I'm sitting in jail cause you didn't tell me you reported the card stolen!" he barked.

"You mean the same way that you didn't tell me that you got what, two kids that you have to pay child support on?" I started. "Or the same way you didnt tell me that I'm basically buying all the clothes on your back you so called modeling? Or how you didn't tell me that you've had three different bitches take you to court for ripping them off? You didn't tell me all that so, why should I tell you what I do with my shit?"

The silence on the phone let me know my answer.

"Yeah that's what the fuck I thought," I smirked. "Well I hope you enjoyed it cause it stops today."

"Yo, I was going to tell you about that shit, but I ain't know how you was going to be able to handle it," he said. "And now you doing exactly what I knew you would. Man you got me in this muthafucka locked up!"

"No nigga using my shit and buying all kind of bullshit got you locked up in jail." I hissed. "You ain't bout to try to flip this shit on

44

me."

"Okay it ain't like I can get you the money back," he pleaded. "But I ain't that nigga that you think I am."

"You ain't got to worry about giving me nothing back." I assured him. "Cause at the end of the day, you ain't getting another dime out of me. You may have played these other bitches, but I'm not the one. So, only thing left for me to say is…don't drop the soap!"

I hung up the phone and that was that. I was cutting all ties with this fool.

This is exactly why my ass was single, because all niggas do is lie. He could try that shit with another chick because I wasn't going to be the one to be his sugar mama.

I changed my number, and my locks just in case his ass made a key, and just as quickly as he came into my life, I had planned on leaving his ass. I was proud of myself.

I got up and smiled. I was feeling good.

Five minutes later I was throwing up into a toilet.

****

Chapter Seven

This had to be the worst day of my fucking life.

I'm sitting in the doctor's office trying to figure out how in the hell my ass is pregnant, and I was taking my birth control faithfully. How could something like this happen? And the fact that it happened with Demetrius of all people.

After everything that had gone down with his ass, I was happy because I felt like I had control of my life. Right after I hung up the phone with him, the shit just hit me like a ton of bricks. Now here I am sitting in this office and this woman is telling me that I'm eight weeks pregnant. She's all smiling but I'm ready to pop her in her mouth.

"I just don't understand." I said. "Explain to me how in the hell I've been taking birth control all of this time and then I still get pregnant."

I guess she could finally see that I wasn't too pleased about it.

"In some rare instances, the birth control can not take full effect," she started to explain. "It's very rare, but, it can happen. Also, there could be other factors that could have prevented the birth control from properly working."

"What the hell does that mean?" I asked. "I take my pill every day at the same time."

"I understand," she nodded. "Out of curiosity, did you drink heavily or do any type of drugs around the time of your conception?"

"No!" I told her.

The fact that she would even ask something like that had me looking at her stupid.

"I'm an occasional drinker, and I don't do any type of drugs." I corrected her. "I have a son already that gets into everything so I'm not trying to have stuff like that lying around even if I did."

"Okay," she recovered. She started looking through my charts. "Well, I see here that you also switched birth control about two months ago."

"Yeah." I answered. "I switched pills because the original pills that I was taking had too much estrogen in it and my cycle was all over the place. My doctor prescribed me a different birth control so that I could regulate my period."

"Well, that could have potentially been one of the factors that caused you to get pregnant unexpectedly," she told me. "If there was a lapse or anything in between, then that's probably what could have triggered it."

My stomach started hurting again and I was trying not to go off.

"But, look at it this way," she smiled. "You've got a beautiful baby on the way."

I faked a smile because I didn't want her to think that I was just being a total bitch.

How the hell can I carry a baby with this nigga? I basically just found out that he was using me. I had his ass locked up, although technically that wasn't my fault, but, still.

The nurse gave me pictures of the ultrasound and scheduled me for another appointment and I left with too many emotions going at one time.

I had some thinking to do. I didn't know if I wanted to keep the baby or not. I didn't believe in abortions, and honestly, it would kill me if I even thought about doing something like that. But, it was too much mess that was keeping me from being happy about it or even wanting it.

He already had two kids that it looked like he wasn't taken care of. If I was going to keep the baby, how do I know he wouldn't try to get me for more than he already had?

I had to really do some serious research on this; starting with talking to his baby mamas.

In the meantime, I needed to keep this pregnancy from Demetrius ass as long as possible. The good thing is, his ass was locked up in jail, and by the looks of it, he wasn't going to be able to afford bail.

On the drive back to the store, I started thinking about everything. Maybe I could take care of the baby by myself. Maybe I could have the baby and give it up for adoption. I didn't know what I wanted to do, but I just didn't want to make a rash decision.

When I got back to the store, I headed right to my office and got back onto my computer. I looked up the women that had put him on child support. I knew it was probably crazy, but I looked them up on Facebook and hit them up asking for them to call me. One of them, Maxine called me right away and it almost seemed like she was happy to talk about him.

"So let me guess," she said when I told her that I'd been dealing with Demetrius. "So you're either knocked up, or you got money and now he done got you all messed up."

"The first." I admitted.

"Girl, you better put that ass on child support real quick," she laughed.

"But he ain't got no money." I said.

"Oh he has money," she corrected me.

"How?" I asked. "He got all these lawsuits that's showing online and barely got a job."

"Yeah," she agreed. "But, he got money. It just ain't in his name. He got a settlement a while back from a little slip and fall or some shit. His mama handles his accounts. When I got pregnant, I filed for child support and got like $50 a month the first time but, then when I found out about that, I took it right to them and they got me my money."

What the fuck? I couldn't believe the shit that I was hearing. If he had this money coming in what the fuck was he doing trying to be a damn Gigolo and shit for? Is he about to be out of money again or something?

"He probably tryna secure some excess funds cause his mama hold that money tighter than a pit bull that got lock jaw," she said as if she could read my thoughts.

"Wow," was all I could say.

"Yeah. Demetrius ass is spoiled," she told me. "For the longest I really thought that we were going to be together and everything. But he's got this thing about using females. His other baby mama she tried to take him for child support, and he played her ass. She's so stuck on stupid she still fucking with him now."

"Excuse me?" I said.

This nigga was fucking me and another bitch but got the nerve to be talking shit about me giving my shit to somebody else?

"Yeah," she continued. "Me and her talk every now and then. I thought she couldn't stand the nigga just like me, but, her stupid ass is still fucking with him to this day because he keeps telling her that he's going to be with her and their daughter and all of his bullshit about being a family. Chile, she believes it. As long as he stays off of child support with her, he going to keep fucking with her. Me personally, I don't want nothing to do with the nigga," she sighed. "Long as he do what he got to do to take care of his son, we cool. How far along are you?"

"Eight weeks." I told her.

"Oh girl you just getting started," she said. "You still got time to handle your business though."

"How old is your son?" I asked being nosey and changing the subject.

I didn't want to be hearing someone tell me to have an abortion.

"He's four," she answered. "And then I think their daughter is like a year old."

"Wow." I said once again.

We talked for a few more minutes before I hung up, and I tried to focus on the paperwork that I had in front of me. I was supposed to be opening my store in a week, but, I was consumed with this and couldn't concentrate.

"So you pregnant huh?"

I looked up and this nigga was standing at the door.

"What the fuck are you doing here?" I growled in disgust.

"You pregnant?" He repeated.

Clearly I needed to fire Erica's ass.

"I asked you a question." I hissed. "What the fuck are you doing here?"

How the hell did I not hear the door open or hear Erica talking to him? Unless her ass was in her damn phone again. Or did he do something to her?

"Shouldn't you still be in jail?" I said.

"I got out yesterday," he told me. "Now answer my question."

"No." I refused. "You need to leave. We ain't got nothing to talk about."

"Obviously we do because you was just on the phone talking about how you eight weeks pregnant and unless your ass is out here hoeing around, then that means you're pregnant with my baby," he said.

This nigga was actually standing here with a smile on his face. Like what the fuck is wrong with him?

"Well just cause I'm pregnant with your baby don't mean I'ma keep it nigga." I snapped.

He frowned and stepped towards me and I jumped up picking my phone up quick.

"Oh please give me a reason to call the cops and have them take

51

your ass back to jail." I warned.

He stopped immediately and stared.

"Don't get rid of my baby Amy. Please," he pleaded.

"How the fuck you gone even form your lips to ask me not to get rid of your bastard child?" I asked. "You already got two kids that you ain't taking care of bro." I pointed out.

He looked like he was beyond uncomfortable and I took pleasure in it.

"Yeah I was just on the phone with your baby mama, and she was telling me how you don't take care of your responsibilities." I continued. "Not to mention how you out here using all these females for money. Who does that? You really think I want to keep this baby knowing that they daddy is basically a low-level pimp?"

"Chill with all that," he growled.

"Uh oh? You mad?" I taunted. "Like I said, you need to be up out of here before I call the police and have them come back on your ass."

"I ain't leaving til we talk about this."

"There ain't shit to talk about!"

Erica came running when she heard me screaming.

"Is everything okay?" she asked looking scared.

"No it is not." I snapped. "Erica why the hell would you let him back here?" I asked.

"Huh? I—I-- I didn't," she stammered. "He came in earlier and was looking at shoes, and I ran to use the restroom real quick. But I told him I would be right back."

"That was stupid as hell." I scolded. "He could have been a robber or murderer or anything. You don't leave customers out on the floor for anything. I done told you that before."

She looked like she was ready to break down but I didn't give a damn.

"As for you," I said turning back to him. "You got five seconds to leave."

I started counting down and he got some sense about him and headed to the door.

"We ain't done. I'll see you later," he told me.

"No you won't." I said.

He walked out of the store, and I turned my attention back to Erica who was standing there crying.

"I am so sorry," she apologized.

I just looked at her and slammed the office door in her face. I knew I shouldn't have snapped on her like that, but this shit was just getting to be too stressful.

I needed to figure out what the hell I was going to do, and fast.

****

Chapter Eight

"Hello?" I answered the phone groggy.

I was probably getting some the best sleep that I had gotten in a while and woke up to my phone ringing.

"When in the hell were you going to tell me that you was pregnant?"

"Huh?" I said snapping out of my comfortable slumber.

I looked at the clock to see that it was a little before six in the morning. Why my mother was screaming into the phone, I don't know.

"You heard what the hell I said. Wake your ass up!" She snapped.

"Mama what are you talking about?" I said trying to tell my brain to wake up and listen.

"Your ass is pregnant!" she yelled.

I heard that loud and clear.

"How did you..."

"It's all over Facebook," she told me. "Your sister came home and said she heard from some little boy that she know that some nigga running around here talking about how you pregnant and thinking about killing his baby. I know that this shit better be a joke Amy Desiree Jenkins," she threatened. "Cause I just know that my daughter is not up in Georgia, knocked up and thinking about having an abortion."

I sat up and sighed listening to her. She was going off on a tangent about a post that she saw. I know this nigga did not go put this shit on Facebook. I should have known this nigga was going to do some shady shit like that the way that he disappeared after he left the store that day.

I hadn't heard from him in a week, so, I figured that he finally got the hint and realized that he wasn't going to get what he wanted from me. But from the way my mama was screaming into the damn phone that lets me know that I was completely wrong.

"So who the hell is this boy?" She asked. "And why in the hell are you even thinking about having an abortion?"

"Mama," I yawned trying to wipe the sleep from my eyes. "It's not how it sounds. He's just being messy because I don't wanna be with him. His name is Demetrius. He actually went to high school with me. We ran into each other about eight months ago, and we started hanging out. But we were never really in a relationship like that because after Thomas, I wasn't trying to rush into a relationship."

"Well obviously you rushed into the bed without a condom!" She snapped. "Cause apparently this boy is on here telling everybody y'all business about how you pregnant tryna kill his baby."

"Can I talk mommy?" I said.

She had me feeling like that same naïve little girl that didn't know anything.

"Go head!" She fussed. "Explain to me why I'm finding out that my daughter is pregnant through other people that are telling me they saw it on Facebook. Explain to me why my daughter didn't even have the common courtesy to pick up the phone and tell me. Or are you actually trying to have this abortion? Cause you know I didn't raise you to kill no babies. If you lay down and made the mistake of spreading your legs to a man that you not even in a relationship with, then you got to own up to your mistakes. Just like you did with that no good Terry. He done messed you all the way up, and now here you go again doing the same dumb stuff."

I just sat there and let her go on. Clearly she wasn't going to let me get a word in edgewise.

I wanted to choke the shit out of Demetrius. It was all his fault.

"You hear me talking to you girl?" She snapped.

"Yes Mama." I replied. "I just…I didn't want to say anything because it was still early in the pregnancy. And you know the first trimester can be the hardest so, until I got past the 12 week mark, I just didn't want to tell anybody."

I knew I was lying, but it was the only thing that I could think of in that moment. It was six in the morning after all.

"Well I hope you know that everybody here is running their mouth about how fast my daughter is and how she out here just having babies with random men," she added.

"Mama I have one son. And I was in a relationship with his father for years. All of a sudden I get pregnant and I'm out here having multiple babies? This is my second child." I pointed out.

"Yeah by some man that you not even in a relationship that don't even respect you cause he put your business on Facebook. And I don't know who you think you raising your voice too, but don't make me reach through this phone and knock you out!" She snapped.

"I'm sorry Mama." I apologized. "But you don't know the whole story."

"I know enough," she argued. "Amy you damn near 30 years old. You can't be running around here making these kind of mistakes. What are you going to tell Junior?"

"I'm gonna tell him that he's going to have a little brother or sister what do you mean?"

"See that's that naive stuff I'm talking about," she huffed. "Amy I meant how are you going to tell him why his brother or sister don't have the same father as him? How are you going to tell him that his brother or sister's father ain't around?"

Shit Terry's ass wasn't around either. I wasn't going to interrupt her though. She was in the zone.

"You got to start making better choices," she ranted. "You need to be a better role model and example for your son. You didn't see me out there running the streets and running wild did you?"

I wanted to remind her that me and my two sisters didn't have the same dad either, but now wasn't the time.

"Mommy I'm doing what I have to do okay?" I said. "I'm not going to let the baby slow me down. I'm not out here tryna spread my legs to anybody. Like I said, I just wasn't in a relationship with this guy. But I've known him for years, and he's just being a little… spiteful right now. But I'm not going to get an abortion."

"You better not," she snapped. "Cause I didn't raise my child that way. And you know God is a forgiving God baby, but at some point in order to be forgiven you got to be worthy of it."

I just rolled my eyes and let her preach.

"Yes ma'am." I said.

There was no way I could get rid of this baby now. Because if I did, I already know my mother would reach through heaven to smack the hell out of me.

"Mommy I got to go back to sleep." I told her yawning again. "I got to get up in like an hour to get Junior ready." I said hoping she was done.

"Well you better fix this and quick," she warned.

"Yes ma'am."

She hung up the phone and before I knew it, I felt the tears. I was stressed out. I was tired, and it only made me hate him even more. He took my choice away from me. Even if I did want to have an abortion, there was no way on God's green earth I would be able to do that.

I cried trying not to wake up Junior, and thinking about how I was going to handle this pregnancy the next seven months. I was pregnant with Demetrius baby, and he was making my life hell. How can I get control of this?

I sniffed and slowly got up out the bed heading downstairs to the living room where my laptop was. I logged on to Facebook and sure enough, I saw where I had all of these comments and tags from people either congratulating me, or saying that they were mad that they didn't know.

How could I do damage control on this? I could just post something saying that it was all a lie. But, then what?

No. I would handle things differently. I had to.

I went back upstairs to lay down, and no sooner had I close my eyes then my phone rang. This time it was Terry.

"What?" I answered blandly.

"So you fuckin some nigga?" He said.

"What business is it of yours Terry?" I asked. "We ain't been together in years bruh. So you ain't got to be questioning me on nothing."

"When it comes to Junior I do," he told me.

I was getting real tired of him using Junior as if he was some excuse or something.

"What the fuck does me being pregnant got to do with you and Junior?" I questioned. "Nigga it ain't your baby so why does it matter? Junior is still taken care of."

"It matters that you done had some nigga around my son."

"Oh you mean a nigga other than his father?" I said.

"You wanted to fuckin move to Georgia. Don't try to put that shit on me," he snapped.

"Yeah. I moved to Georgia." I said. "So what? You act like I moved to California or some shit. Bruh you can get up and come here anytime you want. You slinging and got all of this money, but at the end of the day he still needs a father in his life. Not just a checkbook. So miss me with all that bullshit. Now unless you want me to go wake up your son so that you can talk to him, I will talk to you later I have to get some sleep. Don't call my phone no more with no bullshit."

I hung up the phone and turned it off. I lay back down but I knew I wasn't going to be able to get any sleep. Not with all of this that's going on.

The alarm clock went off, and it took me a few minutes to get up, but, I did. After getting Junior dress, I figured I might as well get the shit over with. I hit up Demetrius and blocked my number.

"We need to talk." I told him.

"So talk," he said.

"I don't appreciate that little stunt you tried to pull." I said.

"And I don't appreciate you trying to kill my baby either."

"Why the fuck do you care all of a sudden?" I pressed. "Did you give a fuck about your other two baby mamas? Cause from what I hear you still fuckin one of them so that she don't put you on child support." I added. "So why you care about wanting to take care of this one? Is that the same thing that you told your other baby mama? Did you tell her that as long as she don't put you on child support that you'll be with her? Is that why you wanted to be with me so bad? Did you get me pregnant on purpose?"

I was rattling off questions faster than they were coming to my mind.

"Yo you need to chill with all of that," he said.

"Oh no." I disputed. "You need to hear this. You took advantage of me. You used me. And you went as low as posting a status on Facebook to try to make me look like I was in the wrong. Newsflash Demetrius. I'm not the one with the fucking record that's available on Google. You are. I'm not the one that got all of these people coming after them for money. You are. I'm not the one that's talking to people at the same time. You are. Or correction. You WERE because I would never go there with you again."

I took a deep breath and continued.

"Now we may be having a baby together, but, that does not mean that you will ever get close to disrespecting me like that." I told him. "You may saw dollar signs with me, but I'm here to tell you, you ain't bout to get rich off of my ass. I worked for what the fuck I got and I ain't about to let some triflin ass nigga like you even think you can touch me. This baby will be taken care of with or without you and if I have to, I will use every dime of my resources to make sure that you don't pull no bullshit like that again. Be clear. We. Are. Done. I will keep you updated as far as appointments and everything like that, and I will do what I have to do as far as letting you see your child, because I'm not the type of chick that is going to keep their child from their father. But the minute that you mess up, the minute that you pull some shit, I will make your life a living hell. Bet on that." I warned.

I hung up the phone before he had a chance to respond and tossed the phone on my bed. That shit felt good. That's what the fuck I needed to do all of this time. When a woman is fed up, she takes control. She becomes empowered. And that's exactly what I was doing. Getting my power back.

****

Chapter Nine

Whoever said that women were the most scandalous people on the planet clearly had never met Demetrius.

It was getting so hard to even have a conversation with him. You would think that he would have taken my warning seriously, but no. This man made it his mission to piss me off.

First, he tried to deny the baby, which was the dumbest thing he could have done. Then, the next thing I know, he's calling my phone telling me that he wants to give the baby his last name. How do you go from denying a baby to wanting to give the baby his last name?

It had been a while since everyone found out and things had calmed down a bit. At this point I was six months pregnant, and, I was miserable. It wasn't necessarily Demetrius making me miserable, it was feeling like I had to prove everybody wrong. I had so many people against me. Demetrius, Terry, my mother.

Things were somewhat better with us but it wasn't something that would happen overnight. She still had a habit of imposing her assumptions unto me. She had come up to Georgia a few times to visit, and we had a heart to heart. She was a big help with Junior which was a load off for me. She had always loved her Ju Ju and had spoiled him rotten so, being there gave me the opportunity to get some rest that I needed.

When I told her everything about the mess with Terry and Thomas, I could tell she was surprised at how I handled it. I wasn't that naïve girl that she thought I was. I think she started to get a better understanding of what I was going through with Demetrius. She told me that I needed to put him on child support, and be done with it. I really didn't need his money, so I didn't think much else of it. Financially, the baby would be taken care of.

I know one thing was for certain, my ass was going to get primary custody of their child. I found out I was having a little girl. I was happy because that's what I wanted. My plan was to have her and then be done. I would have my boy and I would have my girl, and there would be no need for a third. I decided to name her Aries.

I was kind of lonely because I didn't really have any prospects when it came to me. It was kind of hard to when I was carrying this big bowling ball in my stomach every day. My priority was Aries and Junior. Besides, I needed to close one door before I opened another one.

Every day I battled with myself on whether or not I should exclude Demetrius completely from her life. Ultimately, I knew what I needed to do, but, I still wanted to try to find the good in people. That's how I was. Even though I had been burned time and time again, I still try to do things the right way because I didn't want my child asking me why they couldn't see their daddy. I was just ready to have the baby so that I could somewhat return to normalcy.

I was helping Junior with his homework when a knock at the door made me get up and waddle. I opened the door to see a young white guy standing on my porch looking into his phone.

"Yes?" I said feeling the urge to pee.

"Yes I'm looking for an Amy Jenkins," he announced.

"That's me." I said holding my belly.

I really had to pee.

"Hello Ms. Jenkins. Sorry to bother you at home but I have something for you."

He reached into a folder and handed me an envelope.

"What's this?" I asked.

"You've been served," he said. "Have a nice day."

He started to walk off and I stood there confused. What the hell just happened? Served? What did I do?

I closed the door walking back to the table and opened the envelope.

"This muthafucka!" I screamed out loud.

"What's wrong mommy?" Junior asked scared.

"Nothing." I answered trying not to let him see me upset. "Baby do me a favor and go to your room for a little bit. Mommy is going to finish helping you with your homework but I need to do something first okay?"

"Okay," he agreed.

He got up and went to his room, and I finished reading the paper. This nigga was actually trying to sue me for full custody of Aries.

I looked at the complaint in shock and disbelief. Are you fucking kidding me? He was actually trying to take me to court for my baby? No this shit had to be a joke.

I called him and he answered after several rings all happy and shit.

"Are you out of your fucking mind?" I spat.

"Hello to you too," he said.

"Nigga fuck you!" I hissed. "You really tryna take me to court and get custody of my child? Have you lost your ever loving fucking mind?"

"No," he answered. "Actually my mind is quite clear thank you."

"Why the hell would you even do some shit like this?" I asked. "You know damn well that you ain't able to take care of a baby."

"I'm pretty sure the judge would think otherwise," he answered smugly. "I have two kids that I'm already taken care of very well."

"Yeah if you mean fucking the baby mama so that she don't put you on child support!" I reminded him. "Nigga your mother controls your money. And if you think I'm just going to let you take my child you are sadly mistaken."

"C'mon Amy," he said. "You and I both know it's best for the baby to live with me since you're so busy raising your son and managing your stores and everything. You're obviously not going to have time to take care of a baby."

"What the hell are you talking about Demetrius?" I spat. "The baby isn't even here yet. I still have three months left into this pregnancy. So, don't sit here and tell me what I can and can't do. I've been taking care of my son by myself all of this time. I'm managing both of my stores quite well. And my baby is healthy."

"And yet I didn't know about two appointments," he revealed. "You kept that from me."

"What appointments did I keep from you?" I hissed. "Every appointment, I call and tell you about. If you don't answer, I leave you a voicemail. Now it's not my fault that you didn't check it."

"Yeah okay whatever. Like I said, the baby will be better with me."

"Yo whatever the hell you're smoking, has to be some strong and powerful shit." I said. "Cause you actually believe that I'm going to give you my daughter."

"Our daughter," he tried correct me.

"Kiss. My. Ass."

I slammed the phone down on the table and paced the floor. This nigga just would not quit! But no more. The gloves were coming off. I tried to be civil. I tried to be cordial. I tried to be nice. That shit was about to fly out the window.

This is why I made boss moves. This is why I took control of my life. Because when motherfuckers try to do shit like this, I was prepared.

I picked up the phone and called a friend of mine who had an amazing lawyer that handled their divorce. She gave me his information, and I gave him a call. After about a 20-minute phone conversation, he had all the information that he needed, and I sent him a check in the mail for his retainer. If Demetrius wanted to play games, then bring it on. The only difference between him and me, is that when I play, I play to win. He thought he would try to get custody and go for child support for the baby, but he was sadly mistaken. Aries was already taken care of. Now it was time for me to sit back and watch.

It didn't take long because week later, Demetrius called extremely pissed off; at least from what I could gather from the voicemail. I didn't answer his calls at the suggestion of my attorney. I knew that if had, I would have fed right into his plan. Not talking to me was helping my case cause the idiot was losing it.

He had gotten served and was wanted in court.

Three weeks later, we were in court, and the judge not only gave me primary custody, but pending a DNA test, Demetrius was going to have to pay child support right along with his other two kids. I had so much proof of his lack of parental skills, not to mention his baby mama Maxine spoke on my behalf.

I smirked watching him fume in the court. He was standing next to his mother who didn't look pleased either. It was cool cause I never like her anyway. When we were in Florida, she was one of those that talked shit all the time. Karma's a bitch now because her fuck up of a son is the one that's always in some shit.

After the judge rendered her decision, I happily waddled out of the courtroom, and could hear her bitching at him the entire way only making it that much sweeter for me.

"I'm getting real tired of cleaning up your messes boy," she fussed. "You need to get yourself together. Otherwise you gone find yourself living in the streets."

Maybe if she had dug in his ass before, he wouldn't be in the shit that he was in now.

After that day, my life became so much easier. Of course, Demetrius continue to contact me, but there was nothing he could do. The judge had made her decision, and I was elated. I wasn't about no bullshit anymore and he was going to know that. I tried to tell him that when it came to games, I played to win. And I won the championship.

****

Chapter Ten

"Okay Amy give me one more good push now. Count of three."

I nodded and braced myself as the nurses held my feet in the stirrups.

"Okay here we go. One, two, three."

I pushed as hard as I could, and seconds later I finally heard that beautiful cry.

It had been a long 17 hours, but Aries was finally here.

Lying back and catching my breath, I smiled as I watched them bring my beautiful baby girl and place her on my chest. I looked at her and my entire world changed. In that moment, I felt so much joy. Despite everything I had been through in making her and the drama filled nine months, she was here.

I wrapped my arms around her and kissed her at the top of her head.

"How you feeling mommy?" One of the nurses asked.

"I feel really good." I said with a smile still gazing at her. "Actually, I feel amazing."

"That is what I love to hear."

In all actuality, my body was screaming from the inside and out, but, mentally I felt greater than I had in a long time. At first, I thought it was just because she was here, but then I realized that it was more to it than that.

In a way, my daughter being born was that self-realization moment, a moment of reflection.

My self-realization reminded me that a lot of times women are categorized as being sneaky and shady, and there are a lot that are. There are those gold diggers that are out fucking and sucking for the money. But, women aren't the only ones that would do anything to get on the come-up. Men can be just as shady. Men can be just as sneaky.

I had to learn this lesson the hard way. I had to learn that just because a woman gets pregnant doesn't necessarily mean that it's on her. When a man sees a woman that has everything together and going good for herself, he's going to do everything that he can to latch onto that.

A man wants a woman that compliments him. A man wants a woman that he can show off. But, when that man isn't on the same level as the woman that he wants, he's going to do everything in his power to make sure that he keeps her all to himself and that he can get everything that he can from her.

It took three different situations for me to learn this.

Terry, although he was financially successful, treated me like I was property. He cheated, and I thought that I could change him. I thought that my being loyal to him was going to be enough.

As I got older, I had to realize that no matter how much you want to see good in the person, you got to be prepared. You got to stay two steps ahead.

Everybody is out for themselves.

They say that women mature faster than men and that's true. We're

69

ready to settle down first. We're ready to start a family. And it's because of that, that a lot of women put up with shit that they don't need to.

Be careful ladies because niggas will play off of that. They know that we're so quick to want to have families, that a lot of times, they'll use our weaknesses to their advantage.

I became a mother before I was ready to because I let somebody use my weakness to their advantage. Even though I wasn't ready to be a mother to Aries, her being here has taught me that even in the midst of a bad situation, boss up. You can still come out on top.

Demetrius thought that he was going to have a hold on me. I got trapped. I got the last laugh. A man may be able to play the game, and they may play it well. But ladies always remember this, we know how to play the game better.

****

Made in the USA
Lexington, KY
15 October 2018